LEADERSHIP IN RESPIRATORY THERAPY

TABLE OF CONTENTS

INTRODUCTION

Leadership in healthcare, especially in the specialized field of respiratory therapy, is critical not only for the effective management of patient care but also for the advancement of the profession itself. In a rapidly evolving healthcare landscape, respiratory therapists, physicians, and nurses play a pivotal role in improving patient outcomes through evidence-based practices, effective communication, and collaborative approaches. This book, Leading Breath: A Comprehensive Guide to Leadership in Respiratory Therapy, is designed to equip healthcare providers with the knowledge and skills necessary to lead effectively in their roles.

The respiratory system is intricate and essential to human life. As healthcare providers, we must understand not only the physiological aspects of respiratory disorders but also the leadership skills required to guide our teams and patients through the complexities of these conditions. This book will delve deep into various aspects of respiratory therapy, from clinical signs and physiological responses to the interpretation of X-rays and treatment protocols, including pharmacological interventions. Each modules aims to highlight the intersection of clinical knowledge and leadership, emphasizing that effective leadership is grounded in a thorough understanding of the subject matter.

This book aims to be a comprehensive guide for healthcare providers striving to enhance their leadership capabilities while delivering exceptional patient care in the field of respiratory therapy. Through informed leadership, we can improve not only individual patient outcomes but also the overall efficacy and integrity of the healthcare system.

MODULE ONE

LESSON: UNDERSTANDING LEADERSHIP IN HEALTHCARE

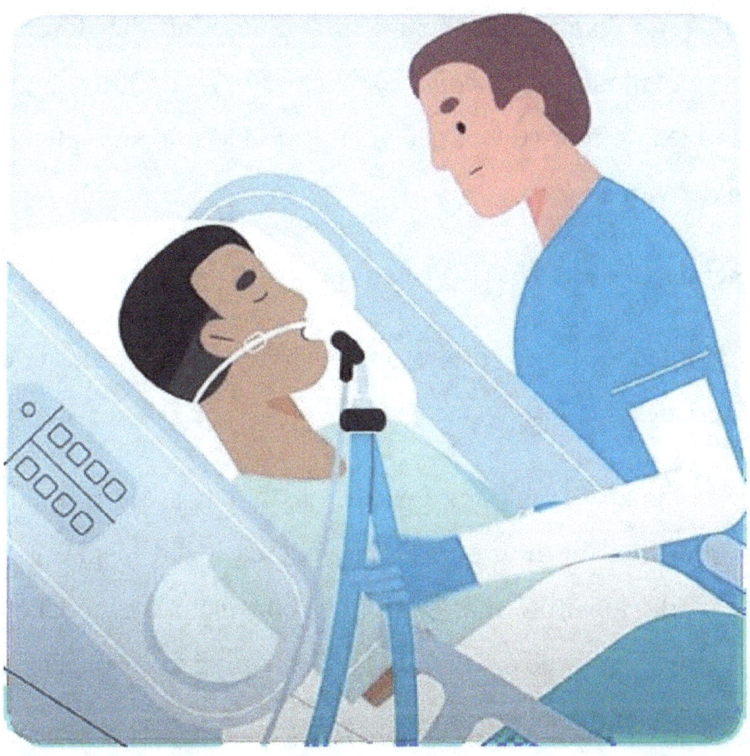

Leadership is an essential aspect of any successful organization, particularly in healthcare, where the stakes are high, and the environment is often high-pressure. In the context of respiratory therapy, leadership plays a crucial role in not only guiding clinical practice but also in shaping the culture and dynamics of healthcare teams. Effective leadership fosters collaboration, enhances communication, and ultimately leads to improved patient outcomes.

Defining Leadership in Respiratory Therapy

Leadership in respiratory therapy encompasses the ability to influence and guide others toward achieving common goals in patient care. It involves a mix of interpersonal skills, clinical expertise, and strategic thinking. As respiratory therapists, we are at the forefront of managing patients with complex respiratory conditions, and our ability to lead effectively can have a profound impact on the quality of care delivered.

Characteristics of Effective Leaders

Effective leaders in respiratory therapy exhibit several key characteristics:

- Visionary Thinking: Leaders should possess the ability to envision the future of respiratory care and inspire others to work towards that vision. This includes understanding emerging trends in the field and adapting to changes in patient needs and healthcare practices.

- Empathy: Understanding the experiences and challenges faced by patients and team members is vital for effective leadership. Empathetic leaders foster an environment of trust and support, encouraging open communication and collaboration.

- Communication Skills: Clear and effective communication is essential in healthcare. Leaders must convey information accurately, listen actively to team members and patients, and facilitate discussions that promote understanding and cooperation.

- Adaptability: The healthcare landscape is constantly evolving. Effective leaders must be flexible and open to change, willing to adjust strategies and practices as needed to ensure optimal patient care.

- Decision-Making Abilities: Leaders are often faced with difficult decisions that can impact patient outcomes. The ability to analyze situations, weigh options, and make informed choices is crucial for effective leadership in respiratory therapy.

The Importance of Teamwork

In respiratory therapy, effective leadership is closely tied to the ability to foster teamwork. Collaborative efforts among respiratory therapists, physicians, nurses, and other healthcare providers are essential for comprehensive patient care. Leaders must encourage a culture of teamwork, where each member's contributions are valued and integrated into the care process.

Strategies for Inspiring and Motivating Teams

- Setting Clear Goals: Leaders should establish clear, measurable goals for their teams, aligning them with the overall objectives of the healthcare organization. When team members understand their roles and how they contribute to larger goals, they are more likely to stay motivated and engaged.

- Providing Opportunities for Professional Development: Investing in the continuous education and training of team members not only enhances their skills but also demonstrates a commitment to their growth. Leaders should encourage participation in workshops, seminars, and certifications related to respiratory therapy.

- Recognizing and Celebrating Achievements: Acknowledging the hard work and accomplishments of team members fosters a positive work environment. Leaders should take the time to celebrate individual and team successes, reinforcing the value of their contributions.

- Encouraging Open Dialogue: Leaders should create an environment where team members feel comfortable expressing their ideas, concerns, and feedback. Regular team meetings and one-on-one check-ins can facilitate open communication and strengthen relationships.

- Modeling Desired Behaviors: Leaders set the tone for their teams through their actions. By modeling integrity, professionalism, and a commitment to patient-centered care, leaders can inspire their teams to emulate these qualities.

<h1 style="text-align:center"><u>MODULE TWO</u></h1>

<u>LESSON: CLINICAL SIGNS: RECOGNIZING PATIENT NEEDS AND LEADING THROUGH SYMPTOMS</u>

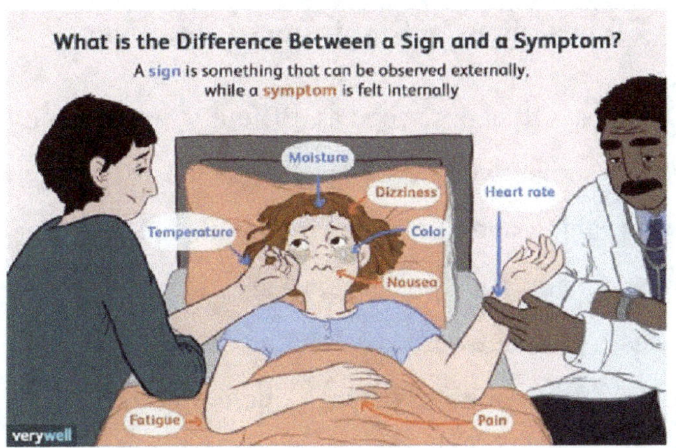

In respiratory therapy, understanding and recognizing clinical signs is paramount to effective patient care and leadership. Clinical signs are observable indicators that reflect the physiological status of patients, guiding healthcare professionals in assessing, diagnosing, and treating respiratory conditions. For leaders in respiratory therapy, the ability to identify these signs is not only essential for patient management but also for fostering a culture of awareness and responsiveness within healthcare teams.

The Importance of Clinical Signs in Respiratory Therapy

Clinical signs serve as critical communication tools that inform healthcare providers about the condition and needs of patients. For respiratory therapists, these signs can indicate the severity of a patient's respiratory distress and the urgency of interventions required. As leaders, respiratory therapists must cultivate an environment where the recognition of clinical signs is prioritized, fostering collaboration and effective decision-making.

Common Clinical Signs in Respiratory Conditions

- Dyspnea: Often described as difficulty breathing, dyspnea can be a subjective experience reported by patients or an observable condition noted by healthcare providers. Leaders must ensure that their teams are trained to recognize and assess dyspnea effectively, as it can indicate various underlying respiratory issues, including asthma, COPD, and pneumonia.

- Cyanosis: This bluish discoloration of the skin and mucous membranes, particularly around the lips and fingertips, indicates inadequate oxygenation. Recognizing cyanosis is crucial for respiratory therapists, as it often necessitates immediate intervention to restore oxygen levels and prevent complications.

- Tachypnea and Bradypnea: Rapid breathing (tachypnea) or abnormally slow breathing (bradypnea) are clinical signs that can reflect various respiratory and metabolic conditions. Leaders should encourage their teams to closely monitor respiratory rates and understand the implications of these signs in the context of the patient's overall clinical picture.

- Use of Accessory Muscles: The recruitment of accessory muscles during respiration indicates increased respiratory effort and potential respiratory distress. Educating teams to observe and interpret this sign can prompt timely interventions, improving patient outcomes.

- Abnormal Lung Sounds: Auscultation reveals various lung sounds, including wheezes, crackles, and stridor, each of which signifies different respiratory conditions. Leaders must advocate for training in auscultation techniques to ensure team members can accurately interpret these sounds and respond appropriately.

Leadership Strategies for Recognizing Clinical Signs

To foster a culture of awareness and responsiveness to clinical signs, leaders in respiratory therapy can implement several strategies:

- Education and Training: Ongoing education is vital in equipping healthcare providers with the skills needed to recognize clinical signs. Leaders should facilitate regular training sessions, workshops, and simulations that emphasize the identification and assessment of respiratory symptoms.

- Clinical Protocols and Guidelines: Establishing standardized clinical protocols for recognizing and responding to common clinical signs can streamline decision-making processes. Leaders should ensure that team members are familiar with these protocols, promoting consistency in patient care.

- Encouraging Collaborative Assessments: Collaborative assessments among healthcare providers enhance the identification of clinical signs. Leaders should foster interdisciplinary teamwork, encouraging respiratory therapists to engage with physicians, nurses, and other specialists in evaluating patient conditions.

- Implementing Technology and Tools: Utilizing technology, such as telehealth and remote monitoring tools, can enhance the detection of clinical signs. Leaders should advocate for the adoption of these technologies, ensuring that teams can leverage them to improve patient assessment and management.

- Fostering Open Communication: A culture of open communication encourages team members to share their observations and concerns regarding clinical signs. Leaders should promote an environment where feedback is welcomed, and team members feel empowered to speak up when they notice significant changes in patient status.

The Role of Leadership in Patient Management

Effective leadership in respiratory therapy involves not only recognizing clinical signs but also understanding how to respond appropriately to these signs in patient management. This includes:

- Prioritizing Patient Assessment: Leaders must emphasize the importance of thorough patient assessments to identify clinical signs early. This proactive approach enables timely interventions, ultimately improving patient outcomes.

- Advocating for Evidence-Based Practices: Leaders should advocate for evidence-based practices in managing respiratory conditions. This includes staying informed about the latest research and guidelines, ensuring that teams apply the most current knowledge in their assessments and interventions.

- Developing Action Plans: Upon recognizing clinical signs, leaders must ensure that teams develop comprehensive action plans that address patient needs. This includes determining the appropriate interventions, medications, and referrals to specialists if necessary.

- Monitoring and Evaluation: Continuous monitoring and evaluation of patient responses to interventions are crucial. Leaders should implement mechanisms for tracking patient progress, facilitating discussions among team members regarding treatment efficacy, and adjusting plans as needed.

- Encouraging Reflection and Learning: Leadership in respiratory therapy involves encouraging a culture of reflection and learning. Leaders should prompt team members to discuss cases, share experiences, and analyze clinical signs to enhance collective knowledge and improve future practices.

MODULE THREE

LESSON: PHYSIOLOGICAL SIGNS: THE UNDERLYING BIOLOGY OF RESPIRATORY DISORDERS

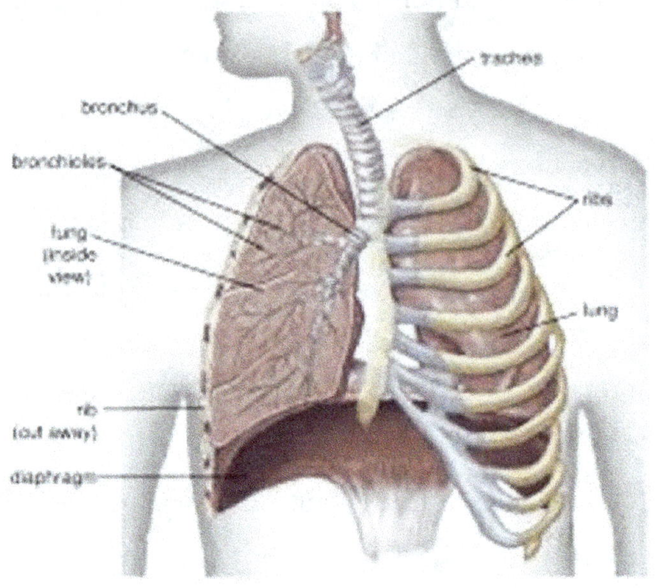

In the realm of respiratory therapy, understanding the physiological signs that accompany respiratory disorders is vital for effective patient management and leadership. Physiological signs are objective measurements and observable indicators of the body's biological responses to respiratory distress, serving as critical data points for assessment, diagnosis, and treatment planning.

The Importance of Physiological Signs

Physiological signs provide healthcare providers with valuable information regarding a patient's respiratory status. They are essential for making informed clinical decisions and leading teams in the management of respiratory conditions. As respiratory therapists, leaders must emphasize the significance of these signs and ensure that their teams are well-equipped to recognize and interpret them.

Common Physiological Signs in Respiratory Disorders

- Oxygen Saturation Levels: Measuring oxygen saturation through pulse oximetry is a fundamental physiological assessment in respiratory therapy. Normal levels range from 95% to 100%. A decline in oxygen saturation may indicate respiratory distress, prompting immediate intervention.

- Arterial Blood Gas (ABG) Analysis: ABG analysis provides crucial information about a patient's respiratory and metabolic status, including partial pressures of oxygen (PaO_2) and carbon dioxide ($PaCO_2$), as well as pH levels. Leaders should encourage their teams to interpret ABG results accurately, using them to guide treatment decisions.

- Respiratory Rate and Pattern: Monitoring the respiratory rate and pattern is essential for assessing a patient's respiratory effort and identifying abnormalities. Increased respiratory rates may indicate hypoxia or metabolic acidosis, while irregular patterns can suggest various underlying conditions.

- Heart Rate and Blood Pressure: Vital signs such as heart rate and blood pressure are integral to understanding a patient's overall health status. Leaders must advocate for regular monitoring of these signs, as they can provide insights into the body's response to respiratory distress.

- Capnography: Measuring the concentration of carbon dioxide in exhaled air through capnography offers insights into ventilation efficiency. Leaders should promote the use of capnography in clinical practice to assess patients' respiratory function and guide interventions.

Leadership Strategies for Recognizing Physiological Signs

To enhance the recognition and interpretation of physiological signs within healthcare teams, leaders in respiratory therapy can implement the following strategies:

- Education and Training: Providing comprehensive education on the significance of physiological signs is essential for building competency within teams. Leaders should facilitate regular training sessions, workshops, and case discussions that emphasize the interpretation of vital signs and ABG results.

- Utilizing Protocols and Algorithms: Establishing standardized protocols and algorithms for interpreting physiological signs can streamline clinical decision-making. Leaders should ensure that team members are familiar with these resources and apply them consistently in practice.

- Promoting Interdisciplinary Collaboration: Collaboration among healthcare providers enhances the recognition of physiological signs. Leaders should foster interdisciplinary teamwork, encouraging respiratory therapists to engage with physicians and nurses in discussing and interpreting physiological data.

- Implementing Technology: Integrating technology into clinical practice can improve the monitoring of physiological signs. Leaders should advocate for the use of advanced monitoring systems that provide real-time data on vital signs and alert teams to significant changes.

- Encouraging a Culture of Inquiry: A culture that encourages team members to question and analyze physiological data fosters continuous learning. Leaders should promote open discussions where team members can share their observations, insights, and concerns regarding patients' physiological signs.

The Role of Leadership in Patient Management

Effective leadership in respiratory therapy involves guiding teams in the interpretation and application of physiological signs for patient management. Key aspects of this leadership role include:

- Prioritizing Comprehensive Assessments: Leaders must emphasize the importance of thorough assessments that incorporate physiological signs. This holistic approach enables healthcare providers to develop a comprehensive understanding of patients' respiratory conditions.

- Advocating for Evidence-Based Practices: Leaders should champion evidence-based practices in interpreting physiological signs. Staying informed about current research and guidelines allows teams to apply the most up-to-date knowledge in their clinical decision-making.

- Developing Actionable Plans: Upon interpreting physiological signs, leaders must guide teams in developing actionable plans that address patient needs. This includes determining appropriate interventions, medications, and referrals as necessary.

- Monitoring Patient Responses: Continuous monitoring of patients' physiological responses to interventions is crucial for effective management. Leaders should implement systems for tracking progress and facilitating discussions among team members regarding treatment effectiveness.

- Fostering Reflection and Continuous Improvement: Leadership involves encouraging a culture of reflection and continuous improvement. Leaders should prompt team members to analyze cases, share experiences, and learn from one another, enhancing collective knowledge and practice.

MODULE FOUR

LESSON: INTERPRETING X-RAYS: VISUAL LEADERSHIP IN CLINICAL DECISION MAKING

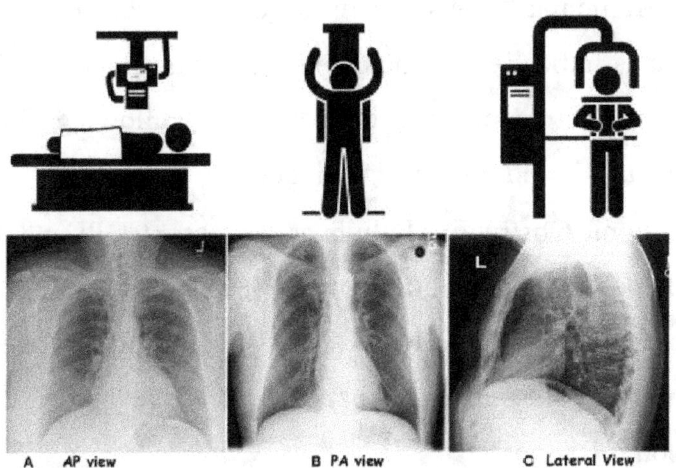

Interpreting X-rays is a critical skill for respiratory therapists and healthcare providers involved in managing respiratory conditions. X-ray imaging offers valuable insights into the structural and functional aspects of the respiratory system, enabling providers to make informed clinical decisions. For leaders in respiratory therapy, understanding how to interpret X-rays and guide teams through this process is essential for effective patient management.

The Importance of X-ray Interpretation

X-ray imaging plays a vital role in diagnosing respiratory disorders, assessing disease severity, and guiding treatment strategies. For respiratory therapists, the ability to interpret X-rays enhances clinical decision-making, ultimately leading to improved patient outcomes.

Leaders must advocate for the integration of X-ray interpretation into the clinical practice of respiratory therapy.

Common Respiratory Conditions Observed on X-rays

- Pneumonia: X-rays can reveal areas of consolidation in the lungs indicative of pneumonia. Leaders should educate their teams on identifying these patterns, allowing for prompt diagnosis and treatment initiation.

- Chronic Obstructive Pulmonary Disease (COPD): X-rays may demonstrate hyperinflation of the lungs and changes in lung structure associated with COPD. Understanding these features helps teams manage patients effectively and anticipate complications.

- Pulmonary Edema: X-rays can show the presence of fluid in the lungs, often indicating heart failure or other underlying conditions. Leaders should guide teams in recognizing these signs to facilitate timely interventions.

- Tumors and Masses: Identifying abnormal masses or lesions on X-rays is crucial for early detection of lung cancer or other malignancies. Leaders must ensure that their teams are trained to interpret these findings accurately.

- Pleural Effusion: X-rays can reveal fluid accumulation in the pleural space. Understanding the characteristics of pleural effusion on X-rays enables teams to initiate appropriate management strategies.

Leadership Strategies for Interpreting X-rays

To enhance the interpretation of X-rays within healthcare teams, leaders in respiratory therapy can implement several strategies:

- Education and Training: Providing education on X-ray interpretation is vital for building competency within teams. Leaders should facilitate workshops and training sessions focused on recognizing common respiratory conditions on X-rays.

- Utilizing Standardized Guidelines: Establishing standardized guidelines for X-ray interpretation can streamline clinical decision-making. Leaders should ensure that team members are familiar with these guidelines and apply them consistently in practice.

- Promoting Collaborative Interpretation: Encouraging collaborative interpretation of X-rays among healthcare providers fosters a comprehensive understanding of patient conditions. Leaders should facilitate interdisciplinary discussions to enhance knowledge sharing.

- Implementing Technology: Integrating advanced imaging technologies can improve the accuracy of X-ray interpretation. Leaders should advocate for the use of digital imaging systems that enhance visualization and analysis of X-ray findings.

- Encouraging Continuous Learning: A culture of continuous learning encourages team members to stay updated on advancements in radiology and imaging interpretation. Leaders should promote participation in relevant conferences and courses.

The Role of Leadership in Clinical Decision Making

Effective leadership in respiratory therapy involves guiding teams in the interpretation of X-rays and incorporating this information into clinical decision-making. Key aspects of this leadership role include:

- Prioritizing Comprehensive Assessments: Leaders must emphasize the importance of comprehensive assessments that integrate X-ray findings with other clinical data. This holistic approach enables healthcare providers to develop a thorough understanding of patients' conditions.

- Advocating for Evidence-Based Practices: Leaders should champion evidence-based practices in X-ray interpretation and management. Staying informed about current research and guidelines allows teams to apply the most up-to-date knowledge in their clinical decision-making.

- Developing Action Plans: Upon interpreting X-rays, leaders must guide teams in developing actionable plans that address patient needs. This includes determining appropriate interventions, referrals, and follow-up imaging as necessary.

- Monitoring Patient Responses: Continuous monitoring of patients' responses to interventions is crucial for effective management. Leaders should implement systems for tracking progress and facilitating discussions among team members regarding treatment effectiveness.

- Fostering Reflection and Continuous Improvement: Leadership involves encouraging a culture of reflection and continuous improvement. Leaders should prompt team members to analyze cases, share experiences, and learn from one another, enhancing collective knowledge and practice.

MODULE FIVE

LESSON: PHARMACOLOGY IN RESPIRATORY THERAPY: LEADERSHIP IN MEDICATION MANAGEMENT

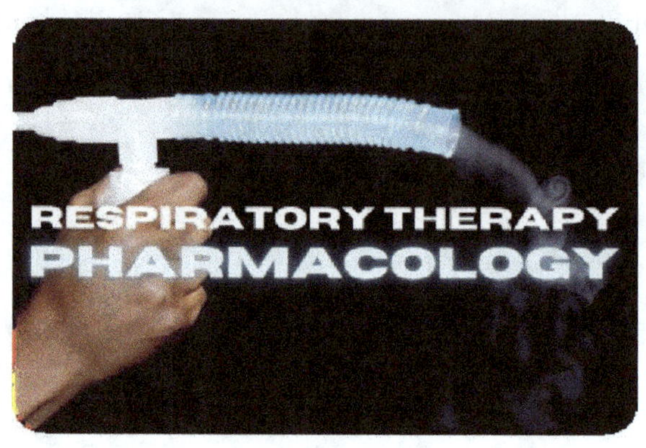

Pharmacology plays a crucial role in respiratory therapy, as medications are often central to managing respiratory conditions. Understanding pharmacological principles, medication types, and their appropriate use is essential for effective patient care. For leaders in respiratory therapy, guiding teams in medication management is vital to ensure safe and effective treatment.

The Importance of Pharmacology in Respiratory Therapy

Pharmacological interventions are fundamental to managing respiratory conditions, from bronchodilators for asthma to corticosteroids for COPD. Leaders in respiratory therapy must emphasize the significance of understanding pharmacology and its implications for patient care.

Key Pharmacological Concepts in Respiratory Therapy

- Mechanism of Action: Understanding how medications work at a physiological level is essential for effective treatment. Leaders should encourage their teams to grasp the mechanisms of commonly used respiratory medications, enabling informed decision-making.

- Medication Classes: Familiarity with different classes of respiratory medications is crucial. Leaders must ensure that teams understand the indications, contraindications, and potential side effects of each medication class.

- Dosing and Administration: Proper dosing and administration of respiratory medications are vital for efficacy and safety. Leaders should advocate for training on dosing guidelines and administration techniques, including inhaler use and nebulization.

- Monitoring and Adverse Effects: Continuous monitoring for adverse effects and medication interactions is essential in respiratory therapy. Leaders must guide teams in recognizing potential side effects and implementing appropriate monitoring protocols.

- Patient Education: Educating patients about their medications fosters adherence and promotes safety. Leaders should advocate for comprehensive patient education that covers medication use, potential side effects, and the importance of adherence.

Leadership Strategies for Pharmacological Management

To enhance pharmacological management within healthcare teams, leaders in respiratory therapy can implement several strategies:

- Education and Training: Providing ongoing education on pharmacological principles and medication management is crucial for building competency within teams. Leaders should facilitate workshops and training sessions that focus on pharmacology relevant to respiratory therapy.

- Utilizing Medication Protocols: Establishing standardized medication protocols for common respiratory conditions can streamline prescribing practices. Leaders should ensure that team members are familiar with these protocols and apply them consistently in practice.

- Promoting Interdisciplinary Collaboration: Encouraging interdisciplinary collaboration enhances medication management. Leaders should facilitate discussions among healthcare providers to integrate diverse perspectives into pharmacological decision-making.

- Implementing Technology: Utilizing electronic health records and medication management systems can improve the accuracy and efficiency of pharmacological interventions. Leaders should advocate for the adoption of these technologies to enhance clinical decision-making.

- Encouraging Patient Involvement: Involving patients in discussions about their medications fosters a sense of ownership and promotes adherence to treatment plans. Leaders should advocate for patient-centered approaches that prioritize shared decision-making.

The Role of Leadership in Medication Management

Effective leadership in respiratory therapy involves guiding teams in pharmacological management. Key aspects of this leadership role include:

- Prioritizing Comprehensive Assessments: Leaders must emphasize the importance of comprehensive assessments that integrate pharmacological data and patient needs. This holistic approach enables healthcare providers to develop tailored medication plans.

- Advocating for Evidence-Based Practices: Leaders should champion evidence-based practices in pharmacological management. Staying informed about current research and guidelines allows teams to apply the most up-to-date knowledge in their clinical decision-making.

- Developing Action Plans: Upon formulating medication plans, leaders must guide teams in developing actionable strategies that address patient needs. This includes determining appropriate interventions, dosing, and monitoring protocols.

- Monitoring Patient Responses: Continuous monitoring of patients' responses to medications is crucial for effective management. Leaders should implement systems for tracking progress and facilitating discussions among team members regarding treatment effectiveness.

- Fostering Reflection and Continuous Improvement: Leadership involves encouraging a culture of reflection and continuous improvement. Leaders should prompt team members to analyze cases, share experiences, and learn from one another, enhancing collective knowledge and practice.

CONCLUSION

Leadership in respiratory therapy is a multifaceted and dynamic role, critical to enhancing patient outcomes, fostering team collaboration, and navigating the evolving healthcare landscape. This book has explored how leadership principles can be integrated into clinical practice, emphasizing the importance of communication, critical thinking, and patient-centered care in shaping effective respiratory therapy teams.

As the field continues to evolve with technological advancements and a growing emphasis on interdisciplinary collaboration and preventive care, the role of leadership becomes even more significant. By embracing innovation, fostering a culture of continuous learning, and prioritizing patient-centered approaches, leaders can guide their teams through the challenges of the future, ensuring that respiratory therapy remains a vital and impactful field.

In conclusion, effective leadership is the foundation of excellence in respiratory therapy. By cultivating leadership skills and staying attuned to the needs of both patients and healthcare teams, respiratory therapists can elevate their practice, improve patient outcomes, and contribute to the advancement of the profession. This book serves as a guide for current and aspiring leaders, offering insights and strategies to navigate the complexities of respiratory care with wisdom, empathy, and a commitment to continuous growth.

<u>REFERENCES</u>

- Day, D. V., Fleenor, J. W., Atwater, L. E., Sturm, R. E., & McKee, R. A. (2014). *"Advances in leader and leadership development: A review of 25 years of research and theory."* The Leadership Quarterly, 25(1), 63-82.

- Ginsburg, L., Castel, E., Tregunno, D., & Norton, P. G. (2014*). "The H-PEPSS: An instrument to measure health professionals' perceptions of patient safety competence at entry into practice."* BMJ Quality & Safety, 23(10), 797-805.

- Heifetz, R. A., & Linsky, M. (2002). *Leadership on the Line: Staying Alive Through the Dangers of Leading. Harvard Business School Press.*

- Hickey, P. A., & Kritek, P. A. (2012). *Leadership for Evidence-Based Innovation in Nursing and Health Professions. Jones & Bartlett Learning.*

- Kohn, L. T., Corrigan, J. M., & Donaldson, M. S. (Eds.). (2000). *To Err Is Human: Building a Safer Health System. National Academy Press.*

- Kouzes, J. M., & Posner, B. Z. (2017). *The Leadership Challenge: How to Make Extraordinary Things Happen in Organizations* (6th ed.). Wiley.

- Leach, L. S., & McAllister, M. (2009). *"Promoting resilience in nurses: Developing emotional literacy through clinical supervision."* Journal of Nursing Management, 17(5), 730-739.

- Manthous, C. A., & Schmidt, G. A. (2016). *"Liberating patients from mechanical ventilation: When and how?"* *Critical Care Clinics.*

- McDonald, K. M., Schultz, E., Albin, L., Pineda, N., Lonhart, J., Sundaram, V., & Malcolm, E. (2014). *Care Coordination Measures Atlas (AHRQ Publication No. 14-0037- EF). Agency for Healthcare Research and Quality.*